AFRICAN-AMERICAN HISTORY

SLAVERY
IN THE UNITED STATES

by Rebecca Rissman

Content Consultant
Ibram X. Kendi, PhD
Assistant Professor, Africana Studies Department
University at Albany, SUNY

Core Library

An Imprint of Abdo Publishing
www.abdopublishing.com

Printed in the United States of America,
North Mankato, Minnesota
022014
092014

THIS BOOK CONTAINS
RECYCLED MATERIALS

Editor: Holly Saari
Series Designer: Becky Daum

Library of Congress Cataloging-in-Publication Data
Rissman, Rebecca.
  Slavery in the United States / by Rebecca Rissman ; content consultant, Ibram H. Rogers, PhD, Assistant Professor, Africana Studies Department, University at Albany, SUNY.
     pages cm. -- (African-American history)
  Includes index.
  ISBN 978-1-62403-148-9
1. Slavery--United States--History--Juvenile literature. 2. African Americans--History--Juvenile literature. I. Title.
  E441.R58 2015
  306.3'620973--dc23
                    2014000106

CONTENTS

CHAPTER ONE

SLAVERY COMES TO THE COLONIES

Settlers from Europe started coming to North America in the early 1600s. They settled along the northeastern coast of what is now the United States. As more settlers arrived, they formed the British colonies. Life in the colonies was hard. The weather and land were very different from the colonists' homelands. The colonists worked hard to grow enough food to survive.

Colonists had to work hard to survive in the New World.

Servants in the Colonies

The colonists needed more laborers to help them work their land. More Europeans came to the colonies. They came as servants. Most volunteered to be servants. They were usually not servants for life. They often worked for other colonists for four to seven years. Then they earned their freedom.

Turning to Slavery

In 1619 a Dutch ship landed in Jamestown, Virginia. Twenty captured Africans were on board. Wealthy colonists bought these first slaves for labor. At first the slaves were treated like servants. They were given the chance to work for their freedom.

Wealthy colonists wanted to grow crops they could sell in Europe. These included tobacco, indigo, and rice.

Native-American Servants

Early colonists tried to use Native Americans as servants. But the Native Americans often ran away. They had a good chance of survival because they knew the land.

Africans were brought to the British colonies against their will.

Such crops needed large fields. The colonists needed even more labor to work these fields. They used both servants and slaves to grow their crops.

Over time colonists worried about losing laborers when servants and slaves earned their freedom. The idea of keeping slaves for life took hold. Slaves could no longer earn their freedom.

Slaves grew and tended to colonists' crops.

The Slave Trade

In the 1630s, a slave trade began in North America in the present-day United States. Ships left countries in Europe loaded with goods to trade. Goods included weapons, material goods, and rum. The ships sailed to the west coast of Africa. Here the goods were traded for African slaves. The European ships packed slaves on board. Then they sailed to South America, Central

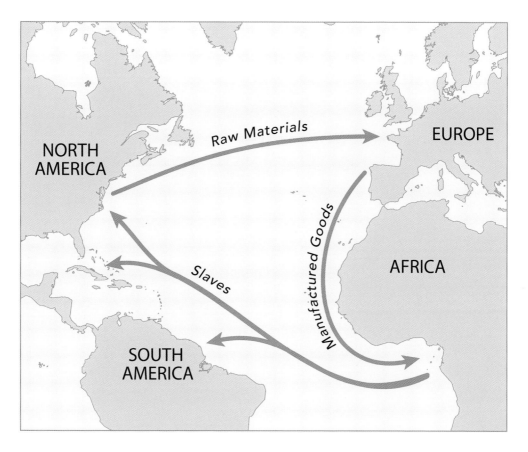

Slave Triangle
This map shows the route of the slave trade. It is known as the slave triangle. How does seeing this map help you better understand how the slave trade worked? Can you see why this route was called the slave triangle?

America, and North America. There the slaves were sold for money or traded for goods. The money and goods were brought back to the European countries. The slave trade cycle continued.

CHAPTER TWO

SLAVERY SPREADS

The journey from Africa across the Atlantic Ocean took months. It was horrible for slaves. They were often chained together. Ship captains loaded as many slaves as possible into all the spaces available. Slaves were allowed onto the decks of the ships only when they were forced to exercise. This was meant to keep the slaves fit enough to sell. Then they were forced back into their cramped spaces.

Slaves were treated horribly on ships and could be whipped by the white crew members.

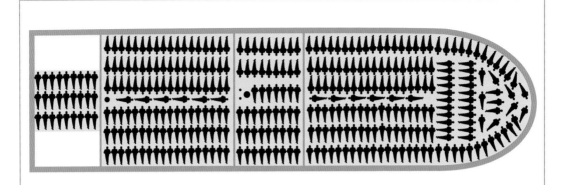

Tightly Packed Slave Ship
Study this drawing of a tightly packed slave ship. How does this diagram compare to the information in the text? How does it help you further understand the conditions slaves faced while crossing the Atlantic?

Unclean living conditions, poor diets, and disease caused many slaves to die before they reached the Americas. Other slaves were so miserable they jumped overboard. Some starved themselves. On some voyages, one-fifth of the slaves died.

Selling Slaves

Once in the colonies, slaves were often sold in public markets. Colonists bid on the slaves. The highest bidder bought the slave. Sick, injured, or weak slaves were brought to shore and sold first. Auctions for healthy, strong slaves took place on board the slave ships. These slaves were more expensive. Ship captains did not want to risk them escaping before they were bought.

Slaves were often separated from family or friends who survived the journey across the ocean. Children were taken from their mothers. Wives and husbands were separated. Usually they would never see each other again.

Farms and Plantations

After the auctions, slaves were moved throughout the colonies. Many slaves worked in big groups on large farms called plantations. Others worked in small groups or alone on farms. Colonists did not have machines to help them raise crops. Slaves grew rice, tobacco, and indigo crops by hand. These crops required lots of manual labor. Having slaves allowed colonists to grow large amounts of these crops. The colonists sold the crops in the colonies and in Europe. Plantation owners became very wealthy because of slave labor.

Family members could be separated if they were sold to different people.

Plantation slaves worked long hours year-round to raise crops. They were often fed very little. On most plantations, overseers supervised slaves. Many overseers beat and whipped slaves. Slaves living on small farms often escaped the horrible treatment of overseers. However, if the farms did not produce enough crops, the slaves might not be fed enough. Some farm slaves starved to death.

Slaves worried about being sold. Slave masters could sell or trade them whenever they wanted. Slaves could quickly lose the life they knew. They could be separated from

Views on Slavery

Colonists believed slavery was acceptable for many reasons. Colonists believed their light skin made them unfit for hard labor in the sun. They believed the dark skin of slaves made them fit for hard work in the sun. Many colonists believed Africans were savages. They were from uncivilized parts of the world. Colonists depended on these reasons to justify their terrible treatment of slaves.

family and friends. They could also be sold to a more cruel or abusive master.

Slave Laws

In 1641 colonists began creating laws to govern the way slaves were bought, sold, and treated. These laws took freedoms away from African slaves. Laws stated slaves were the property of their owners. Colonists could keep the slaves and their children for life. This meant that buying one slave guaranteed generations of labor.

Slaves could not own weapons or travel without permission from their masters. Slaves were punished if they disobeyed their masters. White slave owners

Slave Revolts

Some slaves resisted the way they were treated by their white masters. Twenty-five slaves revolted in 1712 in New York City. They killed nine white people. In 1739 approximately 80 slaves revolted in Stono, South Carolina. They killed 21 whites. In both revolts, many participating slaves were killed or harshly punished.

Some plantation owners had dozens of slaves.

would not be punished for killing their slaves. But slaves could not physically harm white people. Finally, the law noted slaves could not gather in groups or be legally married. Slave laws made it clear that slaves had no rights. They lived at the mercy of their masters.

Slavery Grows

Slavery spread throughout the colonies. Slaves in the northern colonies worked in people's homes. They also worked as laborers in the cities. But slavery was most common in the South. Southern colonies had many farms and plantations that needed many laborers. Slave labor helped build the economies of the colonies, especially in the South.

Olaudah Equiano was enslaved as a child in the mid-1700s. He was able buy his freedom later in life. In *The Interesting Narrative of the Life of Olaudah Equiano, Or Gustavus Vassa, the African*, he wrote about his experience in a slave ship:

> I was soon put down under the decks, and there I received such a salutation in my nostrils as I had never experienced in my life: so that, with the loathsomeness of the stench, and crying together, I became so sick and low that I was not able to eat, nor had I the least desire to taste any thing. I now wished for the last friend, death, to relieve me; but soon, to my grief, two of the white men offered me eatables; and, on my refusing to eat, one of them held me fast by the hands, and laid me across I think the windlass, and tied my feet, while the other flogged me severely.

Source: Olaudah Equiano. The Interesting Narrative of the Life of Olaudah Equiano, Or Gustavus Vassa. *London: Olaudah Equiano, 1794.* Google Book Search. *Web.* Accessed June 17, 2013.

Point of View

This text is told from the point of view of a frightened and abused African. How would the text be different if the slave ship's captain described the ship? Write a short essay that describes the ship's conditions from the captain's view. Then compare the two points of view.

CHAPTER THREE

A NATION DIVIDED

On July 4, 1776, the British colonies announced in the Declaration of Independence that they were free from British rule. This document stated the colonies were a new country, the United States of America. For the next seven years, Americans fought for their independence in the Revolutionary War. In 1783 they defeated the British. They were officially free from British rule.

After becoming its own country, the United States needed to address the issue of slavery.

The North Questions Slavery

The United States needed to create a new government. Slavery would need to be addressed. How would the new country view slavery? Many of the northern states wanted to gradually abolish slavery.

The northern states did not need slave labor for work. Their economy was based on manufacturing and small farms.

The economy in the southern states relied on slave labor. Tobacco, rice, and indigo provided the southern states with large amounts of income. Without slavery, plantation owners

Founding Fathers Owned Slaves

Thomas Jefferson criticized Great Britain's role in the slave trade in an early draft of the Declaration of Independence. He called it "a cruel war against human nature." This statement was taken out of the final draft of the document. At the time, slavery was present in all 13 colonies. Most of the men who worked on the Declaration of Independence were slave owners. This included Jefferson.

Small farms in the North did not rely on slave labor.

believed they would not be able to produce as many crops. Southerners would not make as much money. Southerners felt strongly that slavery should stay. The issue began to divide the North and South.

The Constitution

In 1787 the US Constitution was written to become the governing document for the United States. The Constitution did not abolish slavery. But it did address another issue relating to slavery. The Constitution declared states would be taxed and represented in Congress according to the number of people living in them. White citizens were counted as one person each. The Constitution stated slaves would be counted as three-fifths of a person. This meant African-American slaves were not thought of as equal citizens in legal or economic matters.

The Constitution also gave Americans the right to reclaim any slaves who had escaped from them. Slaves who ran away to the more accepting states of the North had no guarantee they would be safe. They could be found and returned to their masters.

Because slaves were possessions, runaway slaves who were caught could be returned to their masters.

The cotton gin led to an increase in the number of slaves in the South.

The Constitution made it clear that slaves were still possessions of their masters.

The Cotton Gin

Eli Whitney was an inventor. He saw that harvesting cotton, a new southern crop, took a lot of time. Seeds had to be separated from the cotton by hand. He also knew that cotton was in demand in Europe. In 1793 he invented the cotton gin. This machine separated seeds from the cotton. The cotton gin completed the task ten times faster than a person could.

FURTHER EVIDENCE

This chapter discusses the birth of the United States. It also discusses the terrible conditions faced by slaves at the time. What is the chapter's main point? What pieces of evidence support this point? Go to the website below to read part of "Appeal," by David Walker. Find a quote that supports the chapter's main point. Does the quote support an existing piece of evidence in the chapter? Or does it add a new one?

David Walker's "Appeal"

www.mycorelibrary.com/slavery-in-the-united-states

With the cotton gin, the cotton industry in the South exploded. In 1791 cotton farms produced 2 million pounds (907,000 kg) of cotton. By 1860 that number rose to 1 billion pounds (454 million kg) a year. This boom in cotton production made southern plantation owners very wealthy. But it also made them want slave labor more than ever before. Slave labor was still needed to grow the plants. The number of slaves brought into the United States increased after the cotton gin was invented.

CHAPTER FOUR

THE ANTISLAVERY MOVEMENT GROWS

B y the early 1800s, more than 1 million slaves lived in the United States. Most slaves lived in southern states. There they worked on plantations and farms. They also worked in homes and factories. Approximately one-fourth of southern citizens owned slaves. But nearly all white southerners

By the 1800s, more southerners than northerners supported slavery.

supported slavery. Many people who could not afford to own slaves hoped to be able to one day.

Northern states did not support slavery. By this time all northern states had passed laws that would end slavery. Slaves from the South who escaped often tried to travel to the North where they could live freely.

The Underground Railroad

Slaves fleeing the South faced many challenges. First they needed to escape from their masters. Then they had to travel hundreds of miles. They could not be seen by law enforcement officers or slave catchers. These people would return the slaves to their masters.

Harriet Tubman

Harriet Tubman was one of the most famous conductors on the Underground Railroad. This was a network of safe houses and people who helped slaves reach freedom in the North. Tubman was an escaped slave. She made 19 trips to the South. She helped more than 300 slaves safely escape to the North. Tubman was brave and smart. She later said she never lost a single passenger.

To stay hidden, slaves fleeing on the Underground Railroad sometimes traveled during the night.

Escaping to the North meant freedom. But it was a very dangerous journey. Slaves who were caught trying to escape were harshly punished.

In the early 1800s, abolitionists worked to end slavery. They organized a network of safe homes. Slaves could hide in these homes during their journeys north. This network was named the Underground Railroad. People who led slaves on the passage were conductors. Station masters helped supply runaway slaves with food, safe shelter, and clothing. They also gave slaves money to pay for train or ship fare to get them out of the South. From 1810 to 1850,

Nat Turner led a slave revolt that eventually resulted in his death.

nearly 100,000 slaves escaped to the North using the Underground Railroad.

Slaves Fight Back

Slaves who did not escape resisted slavery in other ways. They slowed down their work pace. They let crops die on purpose. Some broke machinery or pretended to be too sick to work. Other slaves killed or stole livestock.

Some slaves organized rebellions. Nat Turner was a slave in Virginia. He organized a large slave revolt in 1831. Nearly 80 slaves attempted to capture weapons stored in Jerusalem, Virginia. They killed at least 57 whites before the US Army stopped the rebellion. The army killed many of the slaves.

The aftermath of this rebellion was nearly as bloody. Slaves in the area were harshly punished, even if they were not involved in the revolt. Many slaves were lynched, or hung by a mob of white people. This rebellion let white masters know how powerful slaves could be. It also showed slaves how terribly they would be punished for acting out.

Riots Erupt

Slave owners and people who supported slavery wanted to stop the abolitionist movement. In 1834 and 1835, abolitionist speakers were violently attacked during riots in New England, Pennsylvania, and New York. William Lloyd Garrison was the publisher of the antislavery newspaper the *Liberator*. During one riot, he was dragged through the streets of Boston at the end of a rope. He had to be rescued by the mayor.

Free African Americans in the North spoke of the need to abolish slavery.

More against Slavery

In the North, the antislavery movement was growing. Abolitionists formed antislavery societies. They wrote letters to Congress asking for slavery to be outlawed. Some people even stopped purchasing goods made by slaves. Abolitionists held conventions and protests. They wanted to inform people that slavery was wrong on moral, religious, and social grounds.

Lincoln Brings New Hope

In 1860 Abraham Lincoln became the sixteenth president of the United States. By this time 4 million slaves lived in the United States. Lincoln was not an abolitionist when he was elected. But he did oppose slavery on moral grounds. He did not want slavery to spread to new territories and states. His election would eventually change the course of slavery in the country.

CHAPTER FIVE

THE END OF SLAVERY

Once Lincoln was elected, tension between the northern and southern states was higher than ever. The North and South strongly disagreed about whether the new territories could have slaves or not. Eleven southern states had seceded from the United States, or Union, by 1861. They created their own country called the Confederate States of America, or the Confederacy. The Confederacy

Southerners did not think it was the federal government's role to decide if new territories or states could have slaves.

Tension between the Union and the Confederacy led to the American Civil War in 1861.

wanted each state to be able to make decisions about slavery. They did not think the federal government should decide if a state could have slaves or not.

The Civil War Begins

In 1861 the American Civil War began between the Union and the Confederacy. The North strongly disagreed with the secession of the South. Northern states wanted the country to stay unified and strong.

Southerners felt the North wanted to change their way of life.

The Emancipation Proclamation

In 1863 Lincoln issued the Emancipation Proclamation. This order stated slaves in the Confederacy were freed. It did not end slavery in the country. But the Emancipation Proclamation reminded people the Civil War was a war for freedom. In 1864 Lincoln was reelected president. He continued to work to end slavery.

Slavery Is Abolished

In 1865 the Confederacy officially surrendered. It had lost the Civil War. Later that year

African-American Soldiers

In 1862 Lincoln declared African Americans could serve in the Union army. Many of these soldiers were proud to fight for freedom and the end of slavery. By the end of the war, approximately 185,000 African-American soldiers fought for the Union. African Americans who did not fight helped support the war. They worked for the Union as carpenters, blacksmiths, cooks, spies, and doctors.

Freed slaves and abolitionists across the country celebrated the abolition of slavery in 1865.

the Thirteenth Amendment was added to the US Constitution. It abolished slavery in all states. The Union had achieved its goals. The nation remained unified. Slavery was outlawed.

Many Americans knew there was still a lot of work to do. Former slaves needed help starting their lives as free people. Attitudes toward African Americans in the North and the South needed to change. Still, African Americans' future looked more promising than it ever had before in the country.

Lincoln's Emancipation Proclamation freed slaves living in the Confederacy. It also stated African Americans could fight in the Union army. Below is a key passage from the proclamation:

> I do order and declare that all persons held as slaves within said designated States, and parts of States, are, and henceforward shall be free; and that the Executive government of the United States, including the military and naval authorities thereof, will recognize and maintain the freedom of said persons. . . .
>
> And I further declare and make known, that such persons of suitable condition, will be received into the armed service of the United States to garrison forts, positions, stations, and other places, and to man vessels of all sorts in said service.

> Source: Abraham Lincoln. "The Emancipation Proclamation." Featured Documents: National Archives & Records Administration. *U.S. National Archives & Records Administration*, n.d. Web. Accessed July 18, 2013.

Consider Your Audience

The Emancipation Proclamation addressed a nation familiar with the conflict of slavery. It also addressed people who wanted to keep slavery. Consider how you would adapt this order for a different audience, such as your classmates. How do you need to change the text, and why? Write a blog post that has this same information for your new audience.

IMPORTANT DATES

1619

The first slaves arrive in the British colonies.

1641

British colonies begin to pass laws that state how slaves are bought, sold, and treated.

1787

The US Constitution states a slave is three-fifths of a person for purposes of taxes and representation in Congress.

1850

By this year, nearly 100,000 southern slaves have escaped to the North on the Underground Railroad.

1860

Approximately 4 million slaves live in the United States.

1860

Abraham Lincoln becomes president of the United States.

1793

Eli Whitney
invents the cotton
gin. This increases
the number of
slaves in the
South.

1829

David Walker
publishes his
antislavery essay
"Appeal."

1831

Nat Turner leads
a slave revolt in
Virginia.

1862

African-American
soldiers are
allowed to fight
in the Union army
during the Civil
War.

1863

The Emancipation
Proclamation
takes effect,
freeing slaves in
the Confederacy.

1865

The Thirteenth
Amendment
abolishes slavery
throughout the
United States.

STOP AND THINK

You Are There

This book discusses the Underground Railroad, which gave many slaves a safe passage to freedom. Imagine you are a slave escaping the South. Write a diary entry about what it's like traveling on the Underground Railroad. What did you think and feel while journeying? Remember to include details about where you slept, who you met, and how you traveled.

Dig Deeper

After reading this book, what questions do you still have about slavery in the United States? Do you want to know about how slaves were treated during the Civil War? Ask a trusted adult to help you learn more about slavery and the Civil War using a reliable website. Write a few sentences about how you did your research and what lessons you learned from it.

Why Do I Care?

It has been more than 100 years since slavery was abolished. In what ways does the amendment still matter? What do you think life would be like today if the Thirteenth Amendment had never been added to the Constitution?

Surprise Me

This book describes slavery in the United States. Learning about slavery can be surprising. Write down three facts about slavery that you did not know before. Read them to a friend. Then explain why you found them surprising.

GLOSSARY

abolish
to officially put an end to
something

abolitionist
a person who worked to
make slavery illegal in the
United States

amendment
an addition or change made
to an existing law or legal
document

auction
a sale where the person who
offers the most money gets
the goods

colony
a territory that has been
settled by people from
another country and is
controlled by that country

constitution
a governing document
that states the rights of
the people and the role of
government

economy
the system of buying, selling,
and making goods and
managing money in an area

overseer
a person who supervises
workers

revolt
to rebel against a
government or authority

secede
to formally leave or withdraw
from a group or union

LEARN MORE

Books

Kamma, Anne. *If You Lived When There Was Slavery in America*. New York: Scholastic, 2004.

Osborne, Linda Barrett. *Traveling the Freedom Road: From Slavery and the Civil War through Reconstruction*. New York: Abrams Books for Young Readers, 2009.

Websites

To learn more about African-American History, visit **booklinks.abdopublishing.com**. These links are routinely monitored and updated to provide the most current information available. Visit **www.mycorelibrary.com** for free additional tools for teachers and students.

INDEX

ABOUT THE AUTHOR

Rebecca Rissman is an award-winning author and editor of children's nonfiction. She has written more than 100 books about history, science, and art. She lives in Portland, Oregon, with her husband and enjoys hiking, yoga, and cooking.